Africa's Origin Stories: The History and Legacy of the Ancient African Stories that Sought to Explain Life

By Charles River Editors

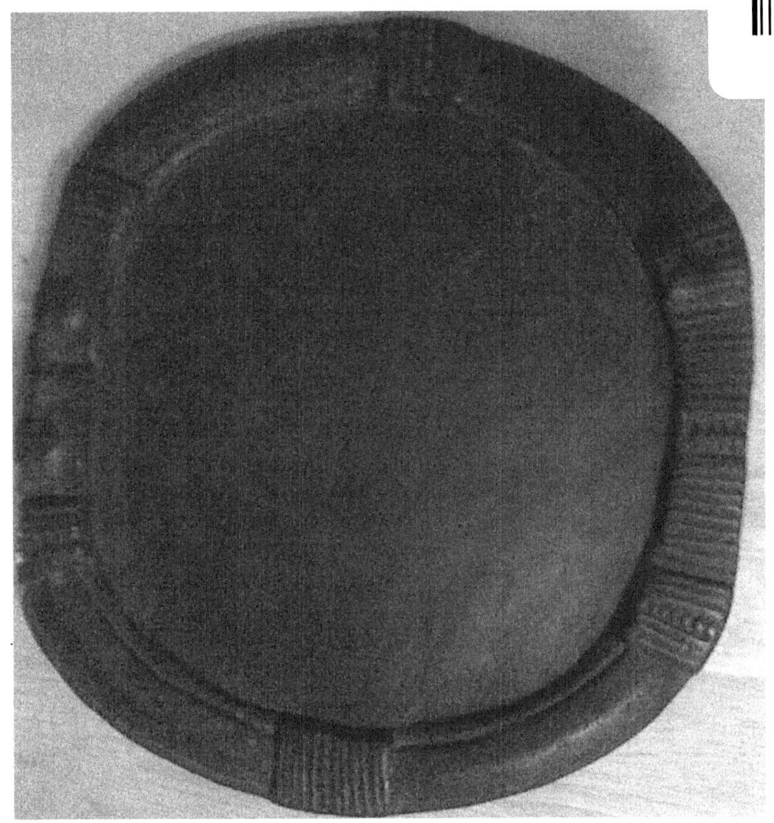

A picture of an early 20th century Yoruba divination board

Charles River Editors is a boutique digital publishing company, specializing in bringing history back to life with educational and engaging books on a wide range of topics. Keep up to date with our new and free offerings with this 5 second sign up on our weekly mailing list, and visit Our Kindle Author Page to see other recently published Kindle titles.

We make these books for you and always want to know our readers' opinions, so we encourage you to leave reviews and look forward to publishing new and exciting titles each week.

Introduction

A picture of Bakonogo masks from Central Africa

In the Lasta Mountains of northern Ethiopia, high on an arid plateau in the foothills, the settlement of Lalibela slumbered for centuries as little more than a pilgrimage site at the end of a long and weary footpath. The ancient trade routes between the Eritrean coast and the central highland redoubts that would later coalesce as the imperial capital of Addis Ababa passed fifty miles to the east of Lalibela, and from the early thirteenth century, after the passing of Gebre Mesqel Lalibela himself, the site slipped into decline. The focus of imperial government shifted south, under the influence of successive emperors, as the holy sites of Roha faded from the popular consciousness. Only the occasional band of pilgrims made the journey over the rugged mountain passes, and across the waterless high valleys to repose at the mythical site, now known only to a handful of faithful acolytes.

The site first came to European attention when it was visited in the early 16th century by the Portuguese explorer Pêro da Covilhã, who struck inland from Zeila on the Somali coast in a quest for the legendary Kingdom of Prester John. He was received by the Emperor Eskender, but he was effectively held a prisoner in Ethiopia for 30 years. During that time, he visited and briefly recorded his impressions of Lalibela.

Also in search of the Kingdom of Prester John was the Portuguese missionary Francisco Álvares, who arrived in Ethiopia in 1515 as part of an ambassadorial mission authorized by the Portuguese King Manuel I. There, in the court of the Emperor Dawit II, he met numerous sundry Europeans, including Pêro da Covilhã, and Nicolò Brancaleon, the Venetian painter who settled in Ethiopia in 1480 and whose artistic influence remains visible in ecclesiastical imagery all over the country.

It was Alvarez who described in detail the monuments of Lalibela in his exhaustive travelogue, *A True Relation of the Lands of Prester John of the Indies*. The explorer wrote, "At a day's journey from this church of Imbra Christo are edifices, the like of which and so many, cannot, as it appears to me, be found in the world. They are churches entirely excavated in the rock, very well hewn. The names of these churches are these: Emanuel, St. Saviour, St. Mary, Holy Cross, St. George, Golgotha, Bethlehem, Marcoreos, the Martyrs. The principal one is Lalibela. This Lalibela, they say, was a King in this same country for eighty years, and he was King before the one before mentioned who was named Abraham. This King ordered these edifices to be made. He does not lie in the church which bears his name, he lies in the church of Golgotha, which is the church of the fewest buildings here."

In 1550, an edition of Alvarez's book was published in Venice by Giovanni Battista Ramusio, the Italian geographer and travel writer. This version included numerous drawings and plans, but who supplied these illustrations remains a mystery. The next known European visitor to the site was Miguel de Castanhoso, a low-ranking soldier in the service of Cristóvão da Gama, a Portuguese diplomat and soldier who led an aggressive but ultimately unsuccessful military crusade into Ethiopia between 1541 and 1543. What took Miguel de Castanhoso to Lalibela is not known, nor were his impressions recorded.

By the dawn of the 17th century, Portuguese influence in Africa fell into decline, and the occasions of European contact with Ethiopia became very few and far between. It would be another three centuries before another European would venture into the holy precincts of Lalibela as part of a British military expedition mounted in 1867. Thus, the "rediscovery" of the remarkable churches and the story of Christianity in Ethiopia would only be recently written.

As that indicates, the modern history of Africa was, until very recently, written on behalf of the indigenous races by the white man, who had forcefully entered the continent during a particularly hubristic and dynamic phase of European history. When they began to arrive in sub-Saharan Africa in the early 16th century, Christian missionaries replaced established animist practices with the tenets of Christianity. This was particularly true for the Catholics who offered a faith promising eternal paradise upon the simple confession of sin. In an age of slavery, disease, and inter-tribal warfare when life was unembellished, brutal, and usually short, this was a particularly seductive message. Add to this the ritual inherent in Catholic worship, the drinking of blood and the eating of flesh, and the susceptibilities of a society defined by elaborate religious rituals, and the conversion succeeded with extraordinary ease.

It is also true that the Catholic spiritual hierarchy reflected the structure of African spiritual life. The first line of African worship is composed of the spirits of passed ancestors whose relationship with the living remains direct and active. This overlapped with the idea of a host of saints endowed with specific functions and responsibilities. At a higher level, the more remote ancestral spirits, those of more than three or four generations past who have merged into the overall spirit of the nation, formed a less definable but powerful presence in day to day life. These spirits easily translate to angels, while the almighty creator, too vast and remote to be understood, conforms to the notion of the one God. The embrace of Christianity and Islam, even today, is not necessarily to the exclusion of ancestral spirits, nor the essentials of witchcraft and sorcery. The precarious security of albino people in east and central Africa, whose body parts are sought after in traditional "medicine," is testimony to the fact that these superstitions are alive and well throughout Africa.

Africa's Origin Stories: The History and Legacy of the Ancient African Stories that Sought to Explain Life examines the various legends, how they formed, the evolution of African beliefs, and how they've affected countless cultures. Along with pictures depicting important people, places, and events, you will learn about African mythology like never before.

Africa's Origin Stories: The History and Legacy of the Ancient African Stories that Sought to Explain Life

About Charles River Editors

Introduction

The Creation Saga

The Sun and the Moon

Animals in African Folklore

The Origins of Fire

Heroes

Fable and Parables

Online Resources

Further Reading

Free Books by Charles River Editors

Discounted Books by Charles River Editors

The Creation Saga

The striking commonalities occurring in natural religions the world over arise from the fact that all peoples have been confronted with the same essential stimulus from the dawn of humanity. The sun and moon, the earth and sky, the elements, the eternal cycle, and the animals of nature all begged the same question to form the great and compound mystery. From this central mystery springs inexplicable systems of veneration and worship that, notwithstanding minor regional variations, possess common themes. The most famous polytheistic society in Africa, the ancient Egyptians, were dominated by Ra, the sun god, who merged with Amun-Ra to form the "Hidden One," the immutable and imponderable god of gods. The notion of a sun god is intuitive, for even the most primitive intelligence can ascertain the central nature of the sun in the cycle of life. Thus, the endowment of that phenomenon with divine properties would seem quite natural.

Africa comprises some 12 million square miles. It is over three times the size of Europe and accounts for 22% of the landmass of the world. A significant percentage of it is desert, including the great sand ocean of the Sahara Desert (covering some 3.5 million square miles), as well as the Namib, Kalahari, Nubian, Turkana, and Somali Deserts, which collectively add a similar area of uninhabited or sparsely inhabited regions to the whole. South of the Sahara, there lies the Sahel, a region of semi-desert, populated largely by pastoral nomads. The tropical regions stretch from the Atlantic coast of West Africa, the Bight of Benin, and through the basin of the Congo River. To the east and south lies the savanna belt, stretching south as far as the southern peninsula. One of the most significant, natural features of Africa is the Great Rift Valley, which commences in the Levant and reaches as far south as the Cape. However, its most recognizable features are the deep valleys and volcanoes of the central Rift, concurrent with modern Tanzania and Kenya, overlapping into the Great Lakes region and the continental divide.

Africa, as is common knowledge today, represents the cradle of humankind in which evolutionary threads of the human species separated from the apes. As the sciences of archaeology and anthropology continues to explore the earliest origins of mankind, fresh finds are still periodically unearthed, including the oldest hominin fossil found in Africa to date, which was unearthed in the deserts of Chad in 2001. The more recent movement and distribution of the human species across the face of Africa is somewhat easier to plot thanks, primarily, to the study of linguistics. To plot this in all of its detail, of course, would be impossible in a work of this size, but one can draw a broad delineation into six major language families. Afroasiatic languages are those spoken throughout North Africa, the Horn of Africa, and parts of the Sahel; the Austronesian languages are those spoken in Madagascar; the Indo-European languages, introduced by European colonists and often the *lingua franca* of large areas today, is usually in pidgin form; the Niger-Congo and Bantu languages are the most widely dispersed; and the Nilo-Saharan languages are spoken in places such as Sudan, Chad, and Mali.

As the Christian religion steadily marched toward domination of the Roman Empire, the symbolism became that of Christ. In Coptic and Ethiopian Christian imagery and iconography in particular, many Ancient Egyptian beliefs were repurposed for the sake of Christianity. This is evident in the enigmatic, 12th century Lalibela Churches of Eastern Ethiopia in which Pagan and Christian symbolism are both freely used at a time when one religion evolved to dominate another. The notion of Christ as the son of God merging with the great and almighty God, the one God, is uncannily similar to the merging of Ra with Amun-Ra to create a higher caste of divinity.

Africa was introduced to Christianity beginning with the Copts of Egypt, which influenced the establishment of Ethiopian Christianity, which manifests today in the Lalibela Churches. As is the case with Abrahamic faiths, their introduction into Pagan lands, those societies practicing shamanism or animism, occurred thanks to an overlap of beliefs and a fundamental compatibility between faiths. Today, Africa is dominated by the Christian faith, introduced in sub-Saharan Africa by European missionaries at the dawn of the imperial era. The cannons of Christianity proved compatible with the fundamentals of African belief structures. Barring the suppression of witchcraft, polygamy, and such devilish practices as drumming and dancing, the missionaries found it surprisingly easy to convert large numbers of black Africans. Historians point to the destruction of indigenous African society as a consequence of slavery and colonization, but many features of modern African Christianity contain strong, residual elements of traditional African religions.

The idea of God as the all-powerful, all-knowing creator of all things is a common enough theme in the African faith for Christian missionaries to make inroads. African folktales, particularly those seeking to explain natural phenomenon such and the sun, moon, and stars, invariably feature the intervention of a supreme being. However, prior to the introduction of Christianity and Islam, the belief in a monotheistic God was an alien notion. This is true insofar as the traditional African view of the supreme being was, and is, naturalistic, but there is always something present at the center of the universe that is singular, all-powerful, and immutable. Notwithstanding numerous, inevitable regional variations and different names, the similarities are often more striking than the differences.

In a nutshell, in the broader, universal sense, the African view of the supreme being is typically vague and ill-formed. The supreme being is almost always remote and dissociated from the more elemental, day-to-day human observances. It is a phenomenon that cannot be understood, and there are so few who still subscribe to animism to waste time trying. The world of ancestral spirits is far more present and immediate, and where a theocracy or priesthood exists to communicate and interpret the message of the supreme being, its work is arcane and beyond the knowledge of common men.

Onyangkopon of Ghana, *Ngai* or Kenya, *Mwari* of Zimbabwe, *Ruwa* of Tanzania, *Nkulungkulu* of South Africa, and a great many others all describe the existence of a supreme being. The presence of this supreme being, as with the Abrahamic God, helps account for the greater facts of creation lying beyond the tangible realities evident to the senses. Numerous names for, and definitions of, "God" have been chronicled by anthropologists over the years, but few if any definitive explanations have been offered as to the nature of that divinity. All that emerges is a head-scratching sense of neither knowing nor being particularly interested in whatever that element might be, but it does not typically intrude in the day to day lives of earthly men and women. The African supreme being is not the God of Islam and Christianity, demanding worship and veneration, but something utterly disinterested in the minutia of universal life; the responsibility of localized phenomenon belongs to a bewildering plethora of natural spirits.

Variations on the mythological character of the supreme being are not only regional but localized, with no two individuals inclined to agree when asked. Even in terms of creation myths, the idea that the supreme being created man alongside all the creatures of the earth, and indeed, the earth itself, is not universal. In the case of *Mulungu,* for example, the common Malawian name for the supreme being, legend tells of that being having asked from where all the beings and creatures wandering the earth have come. In other versions, the human species emerged from some spontaneous generation, while the animals are referred to as "*Mulungu's* people" in contradistinction from mankind.[1] Sometimes, the name of this supreme being is the same as the name for death. Not infrequently, death as a phenomenon is in some way connected to the work of a supreme being.

---

[1] Werner 1925:117

All of this leads to the matter of creation myths and stories which vary enormously from place to place and culture to culture. The creation myths and stories of Africa are so many and varied that we can only touch on a handful here. Most, in one way or another, are formed by the natural elements in existence around an individual people or interlinked group of peoples. The Nile, for example, obviously informed the ancient mythology of Egypt, and Mount Kilimanjaro influenced the creation myth of the *WaChagga* people of northeastern Tanzania.

The most widely distributed African language group by far is that of the Bantu. The story of the Bantus' dispersal is one of the most interesting sagas of African history. In a phenomenon known as the Bantu Migration, or as modern anthropology tends to prefer, the Bantu Expansion, the Bantu race radiated outward from its source to dominate much of Africa by way of incremental migration over hundreds of years. It would, perhaps, be fair to remark that most outsiders think of an "African" in terms of the typical "Negroid" or "Congoid" type, making up the vast preponderance of African population. These are the Bantu.

The Bantu originate in the region of the Niger Delta, bordering modern Nigeria and Cameroon. Sometime around 1,000 to 2,000 BCE, pressures on land and the later development of Iron Age technology prompted a steady, outward expansion. In its simplest terms, the movement spread west and north but more vigorously east and south, moving first to occupy the central regions of the Congo Basin before crossing the continental divide and entering the conduit of the Great Rift Valley. This channeled the migrations north and south, eventually distributing the Bantu language across most of east-central Africa and vast swaths of the south. During the course of this advance, more ancient Neolithic races were displaced, absorbed, or assimilated. The only significant surviving example of this are the Bushmen or *San* of southern Africa who took refuge in the arid west of the subcontinent, where small pockets survive to this day.

It is estimated that over 1,000 distinct languages are spoken in Africa, with many thousands of associated dialects. The Congo, the largest African country, is home to over 325 distinct languages and many more dialects. Often, the original Bantu root was shaped by more ancient languages, and certainly, the modern languages of South Africa show the strong influence of the "click" style of the *San*. Then, there are languages such as Swahili, a Bantu language at its root, but influenced by Arabic and Indian vernacular introduced through international trade with the east coast of Africa. It was used as the Swahili lingua franca of trade in vast regions of the interior and dispersed the language as a common medium of communication, often as a second or third language, across most of Africa's east-central region.

This southward movement of the Bantu brought with it peculiar myths and legends associated with the ancient origins of the race, with many more gathered along the way. As a consequence, the mythology and folklore of Africa are dominated by Bantu tales and legends.

The regional concentration of cultural mythology tends to follow the density of population, and the most significant concentrations of the population have historically been in the tropical regions. Anthropologists have also noted that forest lifestyles and experiences tend to generate a particularly dense and vibrant mythology over time, associated with the far greater diversity of life pervading the forest. Forests also tend to limit physical vision, and in a world of deep recesses, dark shadows, and such a diversity of natural form, nature spirits proliferate with equal abandon. West and Central Africa are known for masks and fetishes. Deeper superstitions emerge among forest communities, and lives tend to be lived in constant intercommunication with unseen spirits of the forest.

Pre-colonized African society was a society in which the history was archived in the tradition of storytellers, and it is through this medium that the mythological foundation of any human society is established. Song and dance also occupy a place in the daily process of life, with specific songs and dances appropriate for each seasonal occupation and every social function in society. The recording of the oral tradition throughout Africa began around the turn of the 20th century and continues to this day, although the density and vivacity of the African oral tradition have faded to remnants under the influence of modernity.

The urge to understand the world and the machinations of nature has always been strong. In Africa, as is the case elsewhere, the creation myth is the central feature of social identity, and there are as many variations of it as there are individual societies and communities within the societies.

Perhaps the most quoted creation myths in encyclopedias of African mythology are those of the Yoruba, one of the principal language groups in modern Nigeria. From the Christianized south to the Islamized north, Nigeria offers up what is perhaps the broadest cultural and ethnic diversity in Africa, possessing a great depth of artistic and literary heritage. This story is told in many versions across Yorubaland, universally beginning with the actions of the Olodumare, or supreme being. Olodumare had two sons, the first, named Obatala, and the second, Odudwa. One day, Olodumare sent his sons to earth, giving them three things to carry: a bag, a hen, and a chameleon.

A common feature of every version of this story is that at the time, the earth was comprised of only water and no land. In more than one version of this tale, divinities accompany Olodumare's sons to Earth to prepare the land or create it on the water's surface. In others, it is discovered that the land is contained within a bag, first in the form of sand upon which a coconut palm is planted, and secondly, black soil within which the first crops are sown. Meanwhile, Obatala, the younger of the two brothers, discovers the coconut palm's ability to produce wine, which he drinks and then falls asleep. Oduduwa, the older brother, opens the bag and discovers the sand, which he spreads around the roots of the palm tree. He then releases the chameleon upon the surface of the sand. With the slow and careful gait of a chameleon, it determines that the beach is good and firm enough to bear weight. Next, the soil is spread out, and the hen is released. As hens are apt to do, she vigorously scratches and worries the soil, spreading it evenly, creating the land.

Soon enough, Oduduwa ventures to test the integrity of the land himself. As he does, Olodumare sends Prosperity down as a gift to him. Prosperity is typically depicted as female who brings with her seeds for cultivation, a bag of cowrie shells for trade, and three iron bars to be forged into knives, axes, and hoes. Thus, Oduduwa emerges as

the first king of Ife, the first kingdom of Yoruba, while
Obatala remains among the palms and becomes a
drunkard.

Nigeria was one of the first regions in Africa to come
under the influence of both Christianity and Islam.
Christianity arrived at the coast with the first missionaries,
while Islam was introduced from the north via trans-
Saharan trade. As a consequence, Nigerian creation myths
were modified under the influence of the Abrahamic
tradition, as the character of traditional supreme beings
were adapted and rationalized to suit the Christian and
Islamic notions of God. In Nigeria, as in every British
colony, individuals on trial or giving testimony in a court
of law swore an oath to one of their traditional deities with
their hand on a Christian Bible.

A variation of the Yoruba creation story follows the
same essential theme, insofar as above there was only sky
and below, only water. The sky was ruled by Olorun
while his wife, the goddess, Olokun, ruled all that was
below. This time, the hero is Obatala, a minor deity who
requested and was granted permission from Olokun to
create the earth for the use of living creatures. Obatala
descended to the earth, bringing with him a gold chain
upon which to climb down to earth, a snail's shell full of
sand, a white hen, a black cat, and a palm nut, all of which
was carried in a bag. The sand was spread, and the white

hen released to scatter it about. Obatala called the place Ife and dug a hole to plant the palm nut. As he waited for a forest of palm trees to grow, he kept company with the black cat with whom he occupied himself, fashioning creatures out of clay. He became drunk on an intoxicating drink made from the palm, and the creatures he had made from clay, the people of the land, were imperfect, as the human race remains today. This angered Olokun who initiated a great flood.

In the savannah regions of the south is the *maShona* nation, a majority tribe in modern Zimbabwe. The term "maShona," it is perhaps worth noting, is not one that necessarily originated within the tribe itself. Today, it stands as an umbrella term for a dispersed group of individual clans and sub-groups, sharing a collective language and many common cultural traits, but who do not regard themselves as a unified people. The name was applied by the second major tribe of Zimbabwe, the *amaNdebele*, a close blood and ideological relative of the Zulu, and until the colonial period, the militarily dominant of the two. The maShona creation story, despite its central commonalities, varies in detail across a spectrum of clans and sub-clans. Nonetheless, the most commonly cited version tells a poignant love story between the earth and the heavens.

Mwari, the supreme being of maShona mythology,

created Mwedzi, or the moon, in a deep pool of water. Characterized as male, Mwedzi implored Mwari to allow him to live on land. To relieve his loneliness, he was sent Hweva, the morning star, to be his wife. This, Mwari agreed to do, upon the understanding that Hweva would return to the firmament after two years. In those two years, Hweva conceived and gave birth to all the vegetation of the world. After two years, Mwedzi returned her to her home in the sky as promised, with profound reluctance. Soon, he was lonely again. This time, Mwari sent him the evening star, Morongo, sometimes Venekatsvimborume, under the same condition: that she must return in two years. Venekatsvimborume, too, conceived, giving birth to all the peace-loving birds, animals, and people of the world. However, when the time came for Morongo to return, Mwedzi would not allow it. Morongo immediately conceived again, this time giving birth to the violent predators: lions, crocodiles, poisonous snakes, and stinging creatures, like scorpions and wasps.

   Mwedzi and Morongo's fate was for both of them to return to the sky, where they continue to reside to this day. The elements of this tale satisfy the question of earth and sky, the former temporal and the latter divine, along with the procreation of good and evil. It also touches on the importance and veneration of water and its divine power for good and evil. Water features prominently in local maShona mythology, an example of which is the initiation required of a novate spirit medium to live underwater for several years before emerging with the inner-vision necessary to communicate with the God and the spirits.

Another example of the curative power of water can be seen in a story explaining the difference between black and white. During the era of colonization, the curses of slavery and inequality were naturally seen in a racial context. Whites, with their overwhelming power of technology, wealth, and moral authority, were seen as blessed by God, while blacks, the subject of oppression, bondage, and misfortune, were seen as weak and cursed. It was told that a pool of cleanliness existed wherein Mwari ordered the people to wash. Those who were fortunate to find the pool full of water emerged white, while those arriving later to find the pool almost empty were only able to wash the palms of their hands and the soles of their feet.

The story of Unkulunkulu, the supreme being of the Zulu, is much simpler, and in some respects, more human, for Unkulunkulu derives from a human form. The Nguni, comprising the Xhosa, Zulu, Ndebele, and Swati sub-groups, are a Bantu people who originate in the eastern quarter of South Africa. The Nguni were widely scattered toward the end of the 18th and early 19th century by the advent of the Zulu wars. As a consequence, Nguni languages are spoken in regions as dispersed as Zimbabwe, Mozambique, and Malawi, with a similar dispersal of Nguni folklore and mythology.

Long ago, as the story goes, the earth existed only in darkness with nothing but a single seed representing life in its latent form. At some point, under ill-explained circumstances, the seed sank into the ground, and from it emerged a vast bed of reeds, known as "Uthanlga", or the source of all things. As time passed, a single reed transmuted into the form of a man, named Unkulunkulu, the "First Man" and creator of all things. In time, other reeds began to grow into men and women. Others grew cattle, fish, and wild animals. These Unkulunkulu plucked off their branches and set free on the land. He then created the mountains, rivers, valleys, wind, rain, sun, and moon. He taught the people to cultivate, cook, hunt, and make fire, and he named each and every creature of the earth.

Thus, Unkulunkulu was, indeed, the first man and the creator of all things, but he remained human. When all of this was complete, he sent out a chameleon to deliver the message to the people that they, like he, would be immortal. The chameleon went about this task very slowly, irritating Unkulunkulu who sent a speedier lizard in his wake to announce the presence of death. The lizard reached the village much sooner, and death has been among the people ever since. As the creator of all things,

Unkulunkulu, remained immortal and divine.

In other versions of the tale, the lizard eavesdrops on chameleon's instructions, and out of envy, rushes ahead to deliver the opposite message. Another interesting aspect of this tale is that early Christians, who were often the first to commit the oral traditions of their converts to written archives, adapted the "messenger of eternal life" role of the chameleon, casting him as a symbol of Jesus Christ, without appreciating the nuance of the chameleon's position in Bantu mythology.

The notion of man having sprung from a plant is a common theme in Bantu mythology. The folklore of the Herero people of Namibia speaks of man springing forth from the "omumborombonga" tree. Other traditions suggest that man emerged from a cave. In societies such as the Nguni for whom cattle form a central social currency, man and cow often appear together. Another feature of Bantu mythology is the tendency for creation stories to dwell on the emergence of their own people without necessarily attempting to explain the creation of mankind as a whole. It was observed by early anthropologists that while the Zulu, Xhosa, and other allied groups coexisted for a period with the San, no effort was made to include the San in their tales of creation. It is possible they did not see the San as human in the same sense as themselves but created along with the wild animals, existing as a species different than man.

   The Bakuba to the north in the Congolese rainforest is a dispersed tribe of the Congolese rainforest, a remnant of what had, at one time, been a powerful and dynastic kingdom dating back to the sixth century. The Bakuba creation myth tells of one great god, Mbombo, who was solely responsible for the creation of the universe. It is a curious tale filled with unexpected and ungodly imagery. Known sometimes as the "Great White Spirit," Mbombo ruled over a world comprised of only water in a universe of darkness in a theme strikingly similar to that of Unkulunkulu. That is, however, where the similarity ends. One day, after a particularly violent gastric upset, Mbombo vomited up the sun, moon, and stars. Suddenly there was light and warmth and from the heat of the sun, clouds rose from the water. As the level of the water dropped, so land began to appear.

   Mbombo vomited again. This time, up came trees, animals, and people. In this way, by successive bouts of stomach upset, Mbombo eventually regurgitated all that is recognizable in the world today. The only product of all of this vomiting that was not benign in nature was lightning, which was so impulsive, unpredictable, and destructive that Mbombo eventually banished it from the earth to live in the sky, where it remains to this day. Lightning was, however, useful for the creation of fire. Exiled beyond the earth, the people were without fire, and Mbombo instructed them how to draw fire from trees. This periodically enraged lightning, causing it to strike the earth on occasion.

A depiction of Mbombo

There are numerous variations on the theme of God's creating man from clay, originating in every corner of the world. In Greek mythology, Prometheus fashioned men from clay, as did the Egyptian god, Khnum. A variation of the Yoruba creation story sees Obatala creating mankind from clay, and similar themes are found in cultures as widely dispersed as the Māori and Inca.

One such tale is told by the Shilluk people, described as a Luo Nilotic people of South Sudan, residing on both banks of the upper Nile. The supreme being of the Shilluk is Juok, who molded all the people of the world from clay. While he was involved in this work of creation, he wondered the world, finding clay in the land of the white man, and from this fashioned the white race. In Egypt, along the banks of the Nile, he encountered red mud from which he made the brown races. Lastly, when finding his way to the land of the Shilluk, he came upon the rich black earth in which all things grow, and from that, he created the black race.

As he sat with a lump of clay before him, Juok thought to himself, "I will give men long legs to run in the shallows while fishing, like the pink flamingos; I will give them long arms to swing a hoe the way a monkey swings a stick; I will give them mouths to eat millet and tongues to sing with; and I will give them eyes to see their food and ears to hear their songs."[2]

Other southern Sudanese variations tell of God baking his clay men and women in a bread oven, leaving them so long they burned, creating the black race. Trying again, anxious not to make the same mistake, he removed them

---

[2] Knappert, Jan. Pelizzoli, Francesca, ill. *Kings, Gods & Spirits from African mythology.* (Schocken Books, New York. 1986) p. 16.

from the oven early, and they were underdone, thus creating the white race. Trying for a third time, he succeeded; from this emerged the terracotta-colored people of the brown race which he considered perfect. They were, as a consequence, permitted to remain in the fertile regions of the Nile.

As was true with the River Nile, the prominent geography of a particular landscape often informed the mythology of the people residing upon it. As has frequently been the case throughout the history of mankind, mountains are endowed with peculiar significance. Wherever a great mountain is present, a deity invariably resides upon it. In Kenya, the Kikuyu deity, Ngai, occupies the summit of Mount Kenya, while Ruwa, the God of the Wachaga people of northeastern Tanzania, lives on Mount Kilimanjaro.

Table Mountain, known to the Khoisan as *Hoerikwaggo,* meaning "mountain in the sea," is the signature feature of the southernmost African city of Cape Town, and the home of Qamata, the supreme being of the Khoi. While busy creating dry land out the sea, a sea dragon, called Nkanyamba, tried to stop him. A great battle followed in which four great giants joined on Qamata's side. When the battle was over and the dragon defeated, the giants were turned to stone, forming the features of the mountain. The largest was given the name Umlindi

Wemingizimu, or "Watcher of the South," and it became Qamata's home.

  The Great Rift Valley is home to Africa's highest mountains and several major lakes, among them Lake Tanganyika, Lake Victoria, and Lake Malawi. Along the eastern shore of Lake Malawi resides a people known as the Yao, a branch of which are also coastal dwellers who have been in contact with Arabic traders for generations. They are, as a consequence, predominantly Muslim, but that does not preclude elements of ancient culture and faith in their folklore and mythology that remain evident today. It is their belief that in the earliest times, their traditional god, Mulungu, lived on the earth in a condition of peace and plenty. Death and cruelty were unknown until one day, a chameleon built a fish trap which he dropped into the river. The following morning, the trap was full of fish, which he ate before returning the trap to the water. Each day, his catch diminished until one day, all he found in the trap was a tiny man and woman. Having never seen such a thing, the chameleon took them to Mulungu who, after examining them, ordered that they be released on the earth to walk around.

  Soon enough, the man and woman grew in stature, and the first thing they did was to strike a flint and start a fire which blazed through the forest. Animals were caught, killed, and cooked on the fire. Astonished at such cruelty and barbarity, the creatures of the earth fled. The chameleon went into a tree, followed by the spider who climbed so high he reached the sky. Mulungu begged to follow and was thrown down a thread of silk upon which he climbed to join the spider. Mulungu fled the earth to escape the brutality of mankind. There, he remained, adding his measure of blame to the maligned chameleon for bringing all of this about.

The chameleon, as we have heard, occupies a unique place in the mythology and superstitions of Africa, in particular among the Bantu. Even today, there are few native Africans who can abide being in the proximity of a chameleon. In many cases, the notion of the chameleon's otherworldly ability to change color and its curious mannerisms are tantamount to witchcraft, as is its role as the deliverer of evil spells. It also brings with it the message of death. A chameleon bite is reputed to have the effect of reversing good fortune, of turning a man into a woman, of inflicting a wound that cannot heal, or of causing madness. The lizard, who carries the message of death, is also despised, but not with quite the same irrational fear as the chameleon. The chameleon is found in the mythology and folklore of almost every African society. While it is almost always a malevolent character, neutral or helpful chameleons are not unheard of though rare. Chameleons can provoke infertility, madness, and melancholy, and when they die, their bones regrow in tiny replicas of themselves.

The Swahili people are perhaps one of the most famous and recognizable of the African races. They are a people of the Indian Ocean coast, stretching from the shores of Somalia to the island of Zanzibar. Their influence on the land and people of east and central Africa has been profound, evidenced by the geographic scope of the Swahili language spoken throughout Tanzania, Kenya, and Tanzania, and in large areas of Somalia, northern Mozambique, Rwanda, Burundi, and much of eastern Congo. Coastal dwellers, the Swahili traditionally acted as middlemen between the Arab and Indian traders of the coast and the vast resources of the interior. Through long exposure, the race is now predominantly Muslim, with considerable inter-breeding and the adoption of an Arab style of life, dress, and worship. The Swahili story of creation is the last one in this section, and predictably, it is an African adaption of ancient Semitic beliefs influencing both the bible and the Qur'an.

At first, there was only God, known as Mungu. God created a light. At first, it was only the dawn, but soon enough, there came the day, with light in all of its majestic spectrum, and He was pleased with the result. Then, in his omnipotence and all-knowing nature, he created everything that was, and all that would ever be. Every human being ever to reside upon the face of the earth was created at that moment, as was every thought, action, fortune, or misfortune until the end of time. First, came the souls of the prophets, the saints, the holy men, and the devout, who would exist only in the glory of Him, decreeing that their souls would reside forever in light. After this, God created the angels. Lastly, the common men and women of the world were created. Then, came the essential elements: the Canopy, the Throne, the Pen, the Book, the Trumpet, Paradise, and Hell.

The Canopy implies the shelter, vast and immutable, beneath which is the Throne. There, God resides in glory. The Pen, which bridges the earth and sky, writes the destiny of mankind, and the Book is the receptacle within which all is written. This is done in order that all men will know and understand the law of God. The Trumpet is to announce the end of days and the time of judgment, opening a pathway for the soul of man either to Paradise or Hellfire.

On a somewhat less orthodox plane, beneath the Throne of God is a tree, known as the "Cedar of the End," the leaves of which are infinite in number, representing the lives of every individual living. When a leaf falls off the tree, it is swept up by an angel, known as Nduli Mtwaa-roho, or the "Reaper of all Souls," and taken to its representation on earth, which is then informed that his or her time has come. The sould is then taken, offering no respite or delay.

After creating the earth and all things on it, God created a cockerel of many colors who stands in heaven and heralds the day, prompting every cockerel on the face of the earth to do the same, inviting the faithful to wake and worship God. With the first crowing of the cockerel of many colors, the sun rises, the day dawns, and the world begins.

The Sun and the Moon

In the elemental world of animist faith, the sun and the moon, with all of the obvious symbolism of life-giving radiance and the unchanging cycles of the seasons, are central. Almost all traditional belief structures in Africa offer up an explanation for the existence of both the sun and the moon, but also the firmament and other imponderables of earth and sky. In times before the generation of electricity and the enlightenment of modern science, when the only light was the sun and moon with their eternal cycle, the mystical relevance of both can hardly be understated.

How the sun, the moon, and the stars arrived on the firmament form a common theme in the folklore of every nation and people in Africa. This is certainly true in Nigeria, which was and remains a favorite of anthropologists and traditional folktale collectors. This is, of course, thanks to the sheer diversity of Nigerian tribal culture, as well as its relative accessibility during the first half of the 20th century, when there was so much work in gathering the African oral tradition. Nigeria was a part of the British Empire, and the British colonies of Africa tended to place a far greater emphasis on anthropological study than the Portuguese, French, Germans, or Belgians.

In Bantu mythology, stories of the sun and moon, in particular, tend to run on the theme of banishment or removal by force. The Bushmen, or San of the Kalahari, for example, although they are not Bantu, explain that the sun lived on earth in a hut. As a consequence, his light shone only in the vicinity of its door. One day, some children hurled him into the sky, and there he remained. The milky way was formed by another mischievous child, throwing hot ashes into the sky. In another tale, it is grains of shining sand. This essential theme, that the sun was thrown into the sky, is echoed throughout Bantu mythology, although it takes on various forms in different regional groups. The idea to that hot ashes thrown from the cooking fire formed the great sweep of the milky way is another common theme.

The Efik people of southeastern Nigeria offer a more elaborate version, commencing with the idea that Sun and Water, as separate elements, lived in a close and harmonic friendship, residing on the surface of the earth. Sun regularly visited Water, though the Water never returned the visit. When the Sun asked Water why he never visited, Water replied that Sun's house was simply not big enough to contain him. Sun scoffed at this and insisted that water come to his home as a guest. Sun, it is perhaps worth noting, was married to Moon, and the two lived in a large compound. One day, as promised, Water paid a visit. With him, he brought all of the sundry creatures of the ocean. As Water had predicted, Sun and Moon were flooded out of their home and crowded by the many creatures living with Water. Sun and Moon were thus forced to flee, taking refuge in the sky where they have remained ever since.

A popular folklore character from West Africa, and Nigeria, in particular, is Anansi, who is typically represented as a spider. The character of Anansi was transported across the Atlantic during the era of slavery and is, consequently, a character appearing in folktales originating from the Caribbean and the Americas. One particular folktale explaining the relationship between the moon, stars, and sun opens with Anansi, on this occasion, apparently represented in human form, and his son, Kweku Tsin, who suffers from a great scarcity of food on land. Kweku Tsin leaves the homestead one morning, as he often does, to try his luck at hunting. He is successful, killing an antelope with his spear. He calls his father to see. Pleased with such good fortune, Anansi instructs his son to watch over the body of the antelope while he returns for a basket in which to carry the meat.

While Anansi is away, Kweku Tsin is visited by a dragon, or a monster of some description, that breathes fire and hungers for human flesh. Kweku Tsin flees, leaving the monster alone with the dead antelope, in which he has no particular interest. When Anansi returns and is told the story by Kweku Tsin, he decides that the pair will hunt the monster. They do not have to wait long, as the monster smells human flesh, finds them, and carries them away to his lair where a great many other unfortunates are being held captive and awaiting consumption.

Kweku Tsin gathers them together and proposes a plan of escape. The others are terrified, knowing the great power of the monster and the loyalty of the white rooster who guards them, crowing loudly the moment at which they try to escape. Forty bags of grain are stored in the larder, and this is scattered across the compound, for Kweku Tsin knows the rooster will not crow if he has grain to occupy his attention. As the rooster obligingly eats, a rope is woven out of hemp, symbolizing, perhaps, the web of a spider. Kweku Tsin proposes hurling the end of the rope into the sky for the gods to catch; it is by this means they will escape.

When the rope is complete, it is flung into the sky where it holds fast, and the captives quickly escape. When the monster discovers the ruse, he scrambles up the rope in pursuit, but once they are safely among the gods, Kweku Tsin cuts the rope, and the monster plunges to his death. So impressed are the gods by this feat that Kweku Tsin is transformed into the sun, Anansi the moon, and the others, the stars.

According to the Yoruba, another Nigerian society rich in cultural narrative, the sun was created by Obatala, son of the sky god. There was once a king of the forest who possessed a beautiful tree of iroko wood, which he neglected to sacrifice to the gods. Irritated by this, Obatala turned the tree into gold and ordered the artisans of heaven to create from it a jar and a boat. Once complete, he ordered his slave, You-don't-hear-what-i-say, to take the golden jar and sail it in the golden boat back and forth across the sky. Thus, the sun came into being. The moon, on the other hand, was created by Olodumare himself, in the form of a flat, round flintstone that spins slowly in the sky, revealing its full form for only three days of the month.

Why the sun is brighter than the moon is explained by the Wuté people of Cameroon in another tale of trickery and deception. The sun and the moon once shone with equal radiance until one day, the sun suggested to the moon that they both bathe in the river. To this, the moon agreed. In the interest of modesty and decorum, the sun suggested he bathe out of sight around a bend, advising the moon that when he saw the water boiling, he would know he had entered. Instead, the sun ordered his children to light a fire and throw embers into the water. As the water steamed and boiled, the moon took his turn. When finally he emerged, his brilliance had been almost entirely quenched. Thus, the sun alone shone brightly in the daytime sky, while the moon crept out only at night.

The moon, however, schemed for revenge. Sometime later, a great famine visited the land, and the moon suggested to the sun that they both kill their wives and children to ease their hunger. To this, the sun agreed, and so, the moon told the sun that he would go upriver to kill his family first, and when the river ran red with their blood, the sun would know it had been done, and he would do likewise to his family. Soon, the sun saw the river flowing red, and he killed his wives and children, throwing their bodies into the water. The moon, however, had simply thrown red clay into the water. This is the reason why the sun shines brilliantly, but it is lonely during the day, while the moon glows softly at night, surrounded by all of the stars who are his children.

Animals in African Folklore

As we have heard, the chameleon is a creature the Africans traditionally regard with fear and suspicion. Other birds, animals, and reptiles are also represented as characters in folklore, according to their peculiarities. The hare, for example, is seen as a nimble and lithe trickster, as is common with many other international cultures. South African native folklore and mythology are particularly rich with allusions to birds. The word for bird in Zulu is *ingonyi*, while in Tswana it is *ngonyani.* In both instances, this translates to "fat" or "fattening" which implies that birds are harbingers of fertility and plenty and with good reason. Migratory birds typically arrive ahead of the first rains, announcing the planting season. A bounty of birds tends to bode well for a bounty of rain which, in turn, promises a year of "fattening."

Birds also carry human souls skyward. They are also receptacles of human spirits that have achieved divine perfection. In times past, certain favored birds were protected, and a proverb in Nguni society warns that to cut a tree harms a bird. The plumage of birds decorated war regalia and the feathers of certain birds, mauve and blue rollers in particular, were reserved only for the use of the king.

A common bird from the South African veldt is a highly

eccentric wader, known as the "hammerkop" or "hammerhead." Like the chameleon, it is a creature bound to attract attention for its curious habits and unusual abilities. It is also a creature deeply revered by indigenous South Africans, some for reasons of wariness and fear, and others in admiration. Among the Zulu, it is regarded as a symbol of human fertility, although elsewhere it is seen as emblematic of vanity and human superficiality. Why it is regarded in either context is a matter of speculation, but some say its expansive and untidy nest must be the home of many offspring. As it stands, searching the wetlands for snails and frogs, it appears to admire itself in the surface of the water.

It is also known as the lightning bird because it is migratory, arriving in the country with the break of the annual monsoon. Because of this, it is often associated with the heavy and violent tropical downpours characterizing the season.

The African Hoopoe, a colorful and companionable bird, is a harbinger of friends, while the lilac-breasted roller, with its palette of blues, lilacs, and mauves, is the bird of peace and reconciliation, often sacrificed by kings when negotiating a truce. Its throat was typically cut with a ceremonial spear, after which the spear was broken by erstwhile enemies.

The list is long, but the holiest of birds in southern Africa is the bateleur eagle. It is also the most beautiful. This visually striking creature is typically seen aloft in the sky or perched among the highest branches of a tree. Its significance varies from place to place, but it is generally seen as representing the beginning and the end or the limitless and omnipresent, and as such, is closely allied to Unkulunkulu himself. The lion is, of course, revered for its courage and wisdom, the snake feared for its malice and poison, the vulture admired for its vision, and the jackal for its cunning. The monkey and baboon usually play the role of the vainglorious buffoon who always get their comeuppance in the end.

The Hottentot or "Coloured" community of South Africa forms a relatively recent sub-culture, nonetheless richly endowed with a folk culture gleaned from both branches of their lineage. Both names are mildly pejorative but remain in wide use today. The rural, Coloured community of the Cape are a people of mixed lineage, typically white and Khoisan, a union dating back to the early establishment of the colony when white women were scarce. They are all that fundamentally remains of the ancient Khoi race of the Cape, and much of their folklore is drawn from that disappeared ancestry and blended with that of the bucolic Cape Dutch who later settled the region.

A typical jackal and monkey story with many variations tells of a jackal creeping into the yard of an old *Boer*, a Dutch rural farmer, and stealing one of his sheep daily. Eventually, the Boer rigs up a "whip," or a spring-loaded noose, which he places in the doorway of the sheep house. That night, the jackal is caught, and the first light of dawn finds him hanging, suspended off the ground. Soon, the Boer comes out and inspects his trap, and that will be the end of the jackal.

It so happens that a monkey is nearby, and when he sees the jackal's predicament, he jumps onto a wall and laughs. "Now, you are caught," he cries, laughing heartily. "And it served you right!"

"Caught?" replies the Jackal. "Caught in what? It is such fun to swing here, up above the ground. I do it all the time. You should try it."

The monkey does not believe a word of it, at least, not in the beginning, but with his appetite for fun, he cannot resist for long. Soon he is scampering across the yard to where the jackal is hanging, and he unties him and ties himself in his place. Just then, the jackal notices the old Boer coming out of his home, and off he runs, laughing.

"It is you!" the Boer bellows when he sees the monkey swinging in the noose, and he lifts his rifle and shoots him.

The jackal is certainly a rare and elusive creature of the veldt, for it is usually nocturnal. His close cousin, the hyena, is diurnal, and always found when some creature has died or is dying. The Hyena is a creature widely despised for its disreputable appearance and manners and its absolute lack of honor and integrity. It is seen as an agent of evil, a deliverer of spells, and the servant of sorcerers and witches. Witches ride on hyenas in the night, sometimes turning themselves into hyenas.

South African folk tales often portray the contradistinction between jackals and hyenas, and one such story concerns an elaborate scheme by a jackal to steal fish. This story is interesting because it deals with non-African themes insofar as it features a wagon. The wheel was not present in South Africa prior to colonization, and this and many other similar tales overlap indigenous and Cape Dutch mythology and folklore.

One day, a jackal noticed a wagon returning from the coast, filled with fish. Jackals are known to be very fond of fish, and it occurred to him that he would like a few for himself. Quick-witted and cunning, the jackal ran a short distance ahead of the wagon, and he laid down as if he were dead. In those days, the silver skin of a jackal was highly valued, so the inert animal was quickly fetched up by the driver and tossed into the back of the wagon. There, he began throwing fish out of the back of the wagon before jumping out himself to return down the track to gather them all up. He discovered that hyena had been following the wagon and had eaten them all. This considerably angered the jackal, and he decided to teach the hyena a lesson.

"You can get all the fish you want," he told the simple animal, explaining the scheme he had used. The next morning, the hyena did exactly as he was told and pretended to be dead on the track, but no one places any particular value on the mange- and flea-ridden pelt of a hyena, and the driver stepped off the wagon and delivered the hyena a sound beating with a club. The hyena remembered the jackal's advice to play dead, and he did. Before long, he was left bleeding and bruised on the side of the track, listening to the jackal's gay laughter as he ran away.

Animal fables and parables populate the landscape of African folklore from one end of the continent to the other, and the broad similarities in theme and meaning are often quite striking. A popular West African tale tells the story of how the chameleon became king. In the days of yore, the animals lived wild, without rulers or laws, and the world was unruly, violent, and wicked as a consequence. One day, the animals gathered in congress to decide that the time had come for them to choose a king from among them. Since nothing like that had ever been attempted before, there were none who knew how it was done. The first and most obvious candidate was Lion, but many of the animals were afraid of him. Next, it was Wild Dog, who suggested himself as a candidate, but the sheep and goats would have none of that, and so it went. Eventually, it became clear that pleasing everyone would be impossible, so another way was suggested. Some distance away, there stood a great stool under a wide tree where some believed the gods to reside. It was decided that a great race would be held, and the first among them to sit on the stool would be the king.

The day of the race came, and the animals set off. Hare streaked ahead and arrived at the stool comfortably ahead of anyone else. As he was about to sit upon it, however, he heard a voice speak, warning that Hare was not the first to sit upon the stool after all. The voice was that of Chameleon, who, unbeknownst to Hare, had ridden on his back, changing color to blend with his coat. When the two animals reached stool and Hare turned to sit upon it, Chameleon simply hopped off of Hare's back.

Hare realized immediately what had happened. He was furious, but the rules of the contest were quite clear: the first to be seated on the stool would be king, and that was Chameleon. As the other animals arrived, they, too, realized they had been tricked. While they had no choice but to declare Chameleon the winner, none among them was prepared to honor him as king.

The Mpongwe people of modern Gabon along the equator tell the tale of why mosquitos buzz. One day, Mosquito and Ear, who were friends, went to take a bath. After her bath, Ear rubbed herself down with sweet-smelling oil, while Mosquito did not. When Ear enquired as to why Mosquito had not rubbed the oil into her skin, which was good for it, Mosquito replied that she had no oil of her own. Ear promised Mosquito some of her oil as soon as she was finished, for she had plenty. However, when she was finished, Ear did not give any oil to Mosquito, who asked angrily why. Ear did nothing but command Hand to chase Mosquito away. Ever since, Mosquito has bothered Ear by incessantly pleading in a high, whining voice for the oil promised to her long ago.

The Origins of Fire

One day, a great hunter was hunting a bright and colorful bird that fascinated him and led him deep into the unknown wilderness. He followed the bird for many days, and although he was unable to kill it, he was aware of a strange cloud rising from the earth in the far distance. Having never seen such a thing, he eventually walked toward it. As darkness fell and the night grew cold, he lost sight of the cloud, but he saw, in its place, the glow of a light. He followed the source of the light and was eventually led to the curious sight of a star lying on the ground, throwing forth hot tongues and crackling angrily. The hunter greeted the phenomenon, and to his surprise, the greeting was returned. He was welcomed and invited to come closer that might share in the warmth through the cold night. In exchange for this, he was asked to feed the flames with branches and logs of wood. This, he did, and he was amazed to watch as the star grew huge.

  The thing then asked if he was hungry, to which he replied that he was. He was instructed to look behind him to see a rabbit. The hunter notched an arrow in his bow and shot it. He prepared to eat the meat raw, as was his custom, but the star suggested he roast the meat over its flames so that he might enjoy it more. While he had never heard of this before, he nonetheless did as he was told and roasted the meat on the tip of his spear. He found that when he ate it, it did, indeed, taste delicious.

  The next morning, the hunter asked the object if he could carry him home with him so that he might have warmth at night and roasted meat every day. This, the flames refused. The star was never meant to travel, never meant to be moved, never meant to have left the place in which God had created him. If he were moved, he would become a danger to man and beast. Moreover, the hunter must tell no-one, for if he did, someone would inevitably seek to steal the star.

To this, the hunter solemnly agreed. With that, he returned home, taking with him some of the roasted meat. When he arrived at home, he gave a little of the meat to his wife. This was certainly a mistake, for thereafter, she demanded more. He visited the star often, keeping it fed and using it to roast meat, and the two became fast friends. The hunter's wife, however, told her friend about the delicious roasted meat and word soon got out. One day, as he left his home to travel to the star, the hunter was followed. As he slept that night, the intruder crept up, seized a burning brand, and ran off with it, trailing behind him a shower of sparks. It was not long before the thief realized that he was being chased by fire, and he dropped the burning brand and fled.

The fire burned the land, dying out only when it had consumed the savanna and all of the villages in it. The villagers saved themselves by crossing a river, but when they returned to their smoldering village, they found their food cooked, their clay pots fired, and much else besides. From that day, the people were respectful of fire, accepting the occasional conflagration in exchange for the opportunity to cook, bake clay, and smelt metals.

Heroes

The stock of African mythological heroes is unsurprisingly wide, with every culture espousing a popular hero, frequently in serialized adventure, and often with a moral.

The Bushmen, or *San*, of the deserts of southwestern Africa, tell numerous tales of Heiseb, of whom we have already heard. Heiseb could be many things, but typically he is portrayed as half man and half God, a traveler across the veld who was conversant in the language of the animals, and whose wife was sometimes described as a beautiful gemsbok.

In the old time, there lived a race of men known as the "Eye-footers" for their curious quality of owning eyes at the ends of their toes. Once, an Eye-footer by the name of Ikaamaegab happened upon a seasonal pool where two sisters were bathing naked. Seizing their clothes, he hid them, and when the two emerged from the water, he refused to return them. One girl, he changed into a tree and was just about to pounce on the other when Heiseb appeared on the scene. The Eye-footer was rather sheepish and agreed meekly when Heiseb suggested that all three spend the night beside the tree that was, of course, the other sister. That night, Heiseb built a fire and they all roasted wild roots and tubers. Heiseb, however, noticed the Eye-footer using his feet to maneuver the best of the food in his direction, and taking a handful of burning ashes, he threw them on the creature's feet, scalding his eyes. With agonized screams, Ikaamaegab ran to the river to ease his pain, and there he became entangled in an underwater vine and drowned.

The next day, Heiseb and the young girl made ready to leave when a voice from the tree was heard pleading not to be left alone. Heiseb ordered the tree to release the girl, and it did, after which the two girls became his wives.

Another popular and rather curious tale of Heiseb tells of his creating the mountains. One day he, a handful of his wives and an infant son were walking across the plains in search of a new home. In those days, the earth had no mountains, and the day was very hot. Soon the little boy was begging to be carried, and so Heiseb lifted him on to his shoulders. At midday, the travelers paused, but when he tried to lift his son off his shoulders, the boy held on so tightly that some of Heiseb's scalp and brain came loose. Undeterred, Heiseb simply collected up the brain-matter, put it in his mouth and blew it into the air, commanding that hills and mountains appear. Next, he took up a piece of his scalp and swung it in all directions, commanding that grass and trees populate the hills, and they did. Then there were cool streams of water running off the hillsides, and forests of trees to shade them. There, in that charming place, Heiseb and his family made their home.

The hero, or perhaps simply the main protagonist, of many a West African tale is Anansi, sometimes portrayed as a man, but more often as a spider, and a curious hero indeed. Anansi is a trickster, not altogether to be trusted, but nonetheless important, for he is the custodian of all knowledge. Tales of Anansi vary widely, and indeed, Anansi is frequently to be found in both Caribbean and African American folklore. The origin of the name "Anansi" is simply the Akan language word for "spider," although across the spread of Anansi folklore, the name has been widely adapted.[3] For example, it has been anglicized somewhat in North America to names such as "Nancy," "Aunt Nancy" or "'Sis' Nancy," all in the female form. Anansi sometimes appears as a pure man, sometimes as a pure spider, but more often as a little bit of both.

Among the slave and maroon societies of the New World, Anansi achieved considerable social relevance, transforming somewhat from the gay and sometimes feckless manipulator of men's emotions and responses to a symbol of slave resistance. Anansi was always able somehow, using his cunning and resourcefulness, often the only method that the slaves themselves had, to prevail, and to occasionally turn the tables on the oppressor.

In a work of this size, it would, of course, be impossible to do justice to all the tales of Anansi, so we will choose instead one or two of the most common. Anansi is the

---

[3] The Akan language is widely spoken in Ghana and surrounding nations.

custodian of all knowledge, and one day, the people of the world offended him, and he decided to seal up all knowledge in a pot, where it would remain until men admitted their folly. In some versions of this story, Anansi seals up all the knowledge of the world in a calabash, simply for the purpose of owning it, and keeping it for himself. Concerned that it was still not safe enough, he decided to secure it at the top of a thorny tree. However, the pot or the calabash was too big and too heavy for Anansi to handle. In some versions, this causes him to realize that the knowledge of the world is too great for one person to manage, and he smashes open the pot to release the knowledge. In other versions, in his attempts to get the pot to the top of the tree, it falls to the ground and smashes. At precisely the same moment, a great storm breaks, washing the knowledge into the streams and rivers, and thus dispersing it throughout the land.

Another tale tells of a time when there were no stories in the world, and so Anansi went to Nyankonpon, the sky god, with the request that he might purchase a handful of stories. Nyankonpon listened to Anansi's curious entreaty, and then asked, when so many other great and good men had tried and failed, why he, a simple spider, thought he could succeed? Anansi replied in his usual way that he was quite confident, and required simply to know the price. To this, Nyankonpon thought deeply before replying that he would consider Onini the python, Osebo the leopard, Mmoatia the fairy and Mmoboro the hornet as a fair price. To this, of course, Anansi agreed.

First Anansi went to the home of the Onini the python, and standing outside, he bethought himself out loud whether the python was indeed as long as a palm branch, as his wife argued, or shorter, as Anansi himself believed. Onini heard and came out to protest that she was indeed longer than a palm branch. To settle the matter, Anansi suggested that she lie beside the palm branch, but this proved unsatisfactory, for Onini could never entirely straighten out. Anansi then suggested that Onini allow herself to be tied to the stick in order to straighten out her curves, and again she agreed. Once safely tied to the palm branch, Anansi quickly carried Onini to the feet of Nyankonpon.

To catch Osebo the leopard was a little more difficult, but Anansi dug a deep pit, and when the leopard fell in it, Anansi offered to help him climb out using his web. Of course, in this way, Osebo became entangled in the web, and he too was carried to the feet of Nyankonpon. To catch the hornets that Mmoboro transformed into, Anansi took a calabash of water which he poured over their nest, and holding a banana leaf over his own head, he cried that it was raining, and if the hornets needed shelter, they might just fly into the empty calabash.

To catch a fairy was a simple matter, for fairies were known to be bad-tempered. He took a doll and covered it with a sticky gum before placing it under the tree of life, where Mmoatia was wont to play. Beside the doll, he placed a plate of delicious yams which no fairy could resist. When she had eaten them all, Mmoatia thanked the doll, who she assumed was their owner, but grew angry when the doll did not reply. Kicking it first with one leg, and then another, she was soon stuck fast.

In this way, Anansi became the owner of all the great stories of the world.

A more conventional hero is Gassire, the hero of the epic tale of "Gassire's Lute." Gassire's Lute is perhaps one of the most sweeping and important articles of West African folklore, originating in Ghana, and first recorded by the German ethnologist and archaeologist Leo Viktor Frobenius. Gassire's Lute is one of a complex of similar epic poems or songs, collectively known as the *Dausi*, associated with the emergence and development of the societies and empires of the Sahel Region.

Gassire's Lute concerns the mythical city of Wagadu, four times destroyed, and four times restored to greatness. Frobenius realized upon making a record of this story that he had stumbled on a significant sequence of the oral history of West Africa. He determined that the four cities portrayed in the epic probably represented the four West African cities of Garama, Ghana, Silla and Agades. These cities, and their associated cultures were linked to the history of Garamantes, an Iron Age culture comprising Berber tribes in the southern region of modern Libya who were known to Herodotus and other Greek and Roman historians. The story perhaps symbolizes the southward migration of the Garamantes to populate the modern states of Burkina Faso, Benin and Niger.

The story of Wagadu begins with the rule of a frail and ageing king called Nganamba in whose place his ambitious son Gassire wished to rule. However, upon consulting a diviner, Gassire was told that he would never rule, but would be a bard, or a lutist, as a consequence of which the great city of Wagadu would be destroyed.

This Gassire refused to accept, and enraged, he condemned the diviner as a liar, to which the diviner simply shrugged and repeated his prediction. Gassire would never be a king but would be a simple musician who would cause the destruction of the city of Wagadu seven times.

The next day, Gassire rode out at the head of his army to do battle with an enemy, returning that evening to announce a great victory. But then, a curious thing happened. Still disturbed by the predictions of the diviner,

Gassire sought solace in the fields, and there he happened upon a large woodcock with an enchanting song which Gassire could clearly understand. The bird was singing the great epic of *Dausi* which Gassire heard for the first time. Gassire was not a sentimental man, but by the song of the woodcock, he was deeply affected, and when it was over, he made his way back home deep in thought.

Thanks to this encounter, Gassire was persuaded that the words of the diviner were indeed true and that his fate was to be a lutist, and so he ordered the greatest instrument maker in the land to build him a lute. However, when handed the instrument, he discovered that it would make no sound, and complaining to the luthier, Gassire was told that only he could make the instrument sing by carrying it into battle and feeding it with blood and horror. Thus, Gassire summoned his eight sons and declared that their names would be legend, and for seven days in succession, great battles were fought. On each occasion, however, one of Gassire's sons was carried home dead, his blood dripping upon the silent lute. Each battle was symbolic of a renewed destruction of Wagadu.

Yearning for peace, the people told their hero to take his last remaining son and leave them in peace. Gassire took his son, his wives and his servants out to the edges of the Sahara Desert, and there, at last, the lute began to sing, and it sang the epic of the *Dausi*. That night his father,

King Nganamba, died, but Gassire would never be king. The Burdama, the enemy, prepared to again attack the city, and without its hero, it fell almost without a fight. The looting and killing was terrible, and the city was left desolate and in ruins.

Leo Frobenius attributed this story to the West African Soninke people, those associated with the empire of Ghana, or Wagadu, and in fact, the word "Gassire" is derived from the word for lutist, singer or "bard."

Gassire features in numerous West African hero tales, and he is, in some respects, the quintessential epic hero, comparable to Hercules, Beowulf or Achilles. According to the 19th-century historian Gerald Massey, the word "hero" itself derives from the Egyptian word *"ma haru,"* meaning true or authentic hero which locates the concept of a mythological hero in Africa. However, the more common encyclopedia entry states that the word is derived from the Greek word *"hērōs,"* meaning "protector" or "defender" which is perhaps more feasible. Yet another school of thought suggests the word derives from "Horus," the name of the Egyptian god of kingship and the sky, who takes the form of a hawk, from where the Greek word probably originates.

As is true in hero myths across the global cultural spectrum, heroes are often derived in part from factual history and in part from legend. One of the great southern African heroes was Shaka Zulu, his name spelt alternately Tshaka, Tchaka or Chaka. While an enormous amount of myth surrounds the existence of Shaka, there is enough verifiable historical detail to construct an accurate chronology of his life. He was born in 1787, and his heroism is derived from the epic of his transformation of a humble and subjugated Nguni clan, the Zulu, to one of the greatest and most feared military empires ever established in sub-Saharan Africa. The phases of Shaka's life conform perfectly to the template of a hero, with only minimal embellishment necessary to offer up the full form of a tribal creation myth.

Shaka was born the illegitimate son of a minor chieftain of the Zulu people and the daughter of a nobleman of a neighboring tribe. His name was that of an intestinal parasite, given to him as symbolic of his despised status and his exile. Historians have since speculated that he was homosexual, and moreover, poorly endowed, which, in a society where boys went naked until puberty, was the source of much mockery and ostracization. He was, however, also highly physical, aggressive and extremely violent. It is also true that he was a military genius, introducing systems and weapons of combat that utterly revolutionized warfare in the region. When his father died, he seized the throne of the Zulu and built up the nation by a combination of relentless warfare, atrocious violence and an unbreakable *esprit de corps* in the ranks of his army.

Shaka's fragile genius morphed inevitably into deep psychosis, and he turned on his own people in a manner that quickly eroded their adoration. In 1828 he was murdered by his brother Dingane, who took over the throne of the Zulu, and who commenced the era of Zulu decline (coinciding with the arrival of European settlers). Shaka Zulu remains the quintessential mythological hero, and a binding agent of a young nation – South Africa – emerging after generations of desperate struggle.

Fable and Parables

It is said in many places in Africa that God made man because he was fond of a good story. African folklore and mythology is replete with fables that offer an entertaining thesis and a practical moral. We have heard a lot so far from one of the great creators of folklore, the Yoruba of Nigeria, but a neighboring group, the Fon of Benin, who fought many wars with the Yoruba, and share many common cultural characteristics, tell the tale of the squabble between Sagbata and Sogbo.

The creator of the universe was Mawu, a goddess who had two sons, Sogbo, who ruled the upper half of the calabash, which was, of course, the sky, and Sagbata, ruler of the lower calabash, which was the Earth. At one time they ruled together, in combination, uniting the two halves of the calabash into one. The two, however, fought bitterly and continuously, and eventually, Sagbata decided that he would abandon his home in the sky and descend to earth, and there live in peace. He demanded, however, that he be given the wealth of his mother which he was due as the eldest son. This his mother would not countenance, insisting that the two must rule the higher and lower worlds as one.

  Sogbo, in the meanwhile, the younger of the two, remained in the sky with his mother and the other gods, and his power, and his exalted position all went to his head. As a consequence, he grew mocking and derisive towards his brother, until eventually, he stopped all rain to the earth, causing a drought that lasted three years. Sagbata was unsure of how to respond but was surprised one day when two creatures of the sky came down to earth carrying in a bag the seeds of prophecy. Such seeds were able to suggest answers to the great questions of the world by the way they fell when tossed. The wisdom that Sagbata required was thus imparted, and he conceded to allow his brother to rule both worlds. After some inevitable gloating, Sogbo accepted this compromise and released the rain, and the earth below became fertile once again.

The story of Sogbo and Sagbata's quarrel has a few variations, and the moral attributed to it concerns the nature of authority, and the dangers of power being concentrated in the hands of one person. It also illustrates the wisdom of compromise.

Many African fables and parables, and there are thousands of them, utilize a cast of animal characters. In a tale similar to the conflict story above, the elephant one day remarked to the rain god that his hubris was unseemly. If he should be so proud of greening the earth, then what would he do if Elephant decided to tear out and destroy all the green things of the earth. To this, the rain god replied simply that he would withhold the rain, and then what would the elephant have to eat? To this, Elephant simply laughed and set to work, destroying all the green things of the earth. True to his promise, the rain god withheld the rain, and, of course, the earth scorched and turned to a desert. Elephant searched the bleak plains for water, digging holes in the dry and dusty riverbeds, until, inevitably, he repented. Sending a grouse into the sky to carry his plea, the elephant begged forgiveness. This the rain god accepted, and the rain fell once more.

The story, however, was not quite over. When a large pool of rainwater collected on the land, Elephant decided he alone would drink from it, and to guard it he assigned the tortoise. Tortoise, however, had no power to stop the

lion who arrived soon afterwards and thus encouraged, the
other animals of the earth approached the pool to drink,
and soon it was all gone. When Elephant returned, he was
quite naturally irritated, and unsatisfied with the tortoise's
plea that he was simply too small and unimportant to
order the likes of Lion about. To punish the little creature,
Elephant brought down his great foot on his back,
cracking Tortoise's shell, and flattening its underside, as it
remains today.

The moral of this story, of course, is multifaceted and is
simply to never defy someone greater than yourself, never
destroy what is vital to you, never assign your valuables to
the protection of a weak guardian, and finally, never be
selfish.

In this story, however, the tortoise is portrayed as the
victim, but the theme of many African fables is the
triumph of the oppressed, and in the elaborate tale of the
Tortoise and the Hunter, this is certainly the case.

There was once a skilful hunter of the Mongo people of
Congo whose daily trips into the forest were always
successful. One day, however, when he had caught and
killed a large antelope, he happened upon a well-known
demon named Claws after the great talons that grew from
his fingertips. The demon appraised the antelope carried
across the hunter's shoulders and demanded that he be

given half. Sensing that discretion might perhaps be the better part of valor, the hunter agreed. This, however, became the demon's daily habit, and before long, the hunter's wife began to notice that only half an animal was brought home every day. Being a jealous type, she suspected that her husband was supporting another woman, and insisted that she accompany him into the forest the next day. However, when the couple met Claws that evening, she fainted with fright, at which Claws licked his lips and complimented the hunter on a fine carcass. Ordering him to section the meat, the hunter protested that the woman was not game, but his wife, and he certainly would not agree to kill her.

After giving the matter some thought, Claws decided that he would seek the advice of his friend Lung-Eater, who agreed to arbitrate only if he could first carve out his own favorite cut. Again the man refused, and this time the question was put to Heart-Eater, who expressed himself pleased to help, but only if he could first slice out his favorite piece. This went on as a succession of demons with names such as Eye-Muncher, Bone-Cruncher and Skin-Chewer arrived on the scene, and eyed the fainted woman hungrily. Eventually, Man-Eater was invited to express his opinion which was simply that the hunter be seized and tied up and his wife killed. This caused the demons to erupt into a bitter argument between themselves, until Man-Eater raised his hands, calling for calm, and suggesting that the matter be put to the wise tortoise Ulu.

Ulu was summoned, and presented with this conundrum, he agreed that the woman should be killed and carved up to be eaten, with him taking his share. Knives were drawn, and the demons advanced, but Ulu stopped them. Tradition demanded, he reminded them, that females be carefully cleaned before slaughter, and for this, he gave the demons baskets to take to the river to collect water. Of course, baskets cannot hold water for long, and each time a demon returned from the river, his basket was empty. This provoked a great deal of consternation among the demons, and as they hurried back and forth to the river, Ulu chewed through the ropes binding the hunter. Gathering up his wife, the hunter thanked the tortoise and fled. To this day the women of the Mongo tribe forswear to eat the meat of the tortoise.

Many African fables contain themes of cunning, hubris and comeuppance, as is true in many parts of the world. The Brer Fox and Brer Rabbit stories of the Uncle Remus books contain moral threads that would be familiar to any listener of traditional African tales. The Nubian tale of the Fox and the Crow is one example, and although originating in the region of the middle Nile, it contains elements common throughout Africa.

A dove was one day sitting on her eggs laid in a nest built high in the branches of a tree. Along came a fox carrying an axe who demanded an egg or else he would chop down the tree and destroy the entire nest. Not wishing this, the dove did as she was told, and down came an egg that the fox caught in his jaws and ate.

Of course, the next day the same thing happened, and again, fearful of losing all of her eggs, the dove dropped one down to the fox. It so happened that a crow was passing, and noticing the dove's soft lamentations, he landed alongside the nest and asked what was the trouble. When he heard the sad tale, he chuckled, for he knew the axe was simply made of clay, and could never chop down a tree. He suggested to the dove that she dare the fox to try, and the next day she did, and sure enough, the fox slunk away, knowing that his axe was simply made of clay.

The fox, however, now nurtured a grievance against the crow, and he was determined to get his revenge. One day he lay down beside the road and pretended to be dead, and since nothing pleases a crow more than a pungent carcass, he landed on the fox's shoulder. In a moment the fox had the crow in his jaws, at which, to the fox's amazement, the crow simply began to laugh.

"I had a dream last night," said Crow. "That exactly this

would happen, and in my dream, you tossed me into the air and my bones and flesh separated and fell to the ground. Why don't you try it?"

The fox did, and sure enough, the crow flew gaily away. The moral, of course, is never underestimate a crow, and never give in to threats.

We cannot conclude this brief look at African fables without another tale of Anansi the spider. Anansi, although an accomplished trickster, can sometimes be the messenger of a sound moral, and according to the Ashanti of Ghana, this did once happen.

This story involves a very bad-tempered and irritable man by the name of Can't-bear-to-be-contradicted who happened one day to fall into conversation with a small antelope known as a duiker, and as they were chatting, a few palm nuts fell from the tree above, and the duiker observed that Can't-bear-to-be-contradicted's nuts were ripe and needed to be harvested.

"Not at all!" replied Can't-bear-to-be-contradicted. "When they ripen, it is three bunches at a time, and from them, I squeeze enough oil to fill three buckets which I use to purchase an old woman who gives birth to my grandmother, who gives birth to my mother who then gives birth to me. When my mother gives birth to me, I am standing right where I am now. What do you think of that?"

"I think you are lying!" replied the duiker, which, of course, made Can't-bear-to-be-contradicted extremely angry, for he could not abide to be gainsaid or contradicted. He was so angry, indeed, that he struck the duiker with a club and killed her. A day or two later, another animal visited, and the same thing happened, and then another, and still another. Eventually, it was Anansi who found his way into Can't-bear-to-be-contradicted's compound, but this time, when the same story was told to him, he agreed that it was absolutely true. What is more, he admitted that at his home he owned a palm nut tree so high that seventy-seven sticks joined end to end could not reach the fruit, but all that he needed to do was lie on his back and he could easily reach the canopy of the tree with his little finger.

Can't-bear-to-be-contradicted laughed derisively but agreed to come to Anansi's compound the following morning to see this for himself.

There are numerous unique elements to this story; for example, the next morning Anansi spilt red palm oil on the path and instructed his children to explain that Anansi injured himself and was forced to go to the blacksmith for treatment. The essential theme, however, is that Anansi, when he returned, instructed his children to cook Can't-bear-to-be-contradicted a meal using as many hot chilies as they could find. When Can't-bear-to-be-contradicted ate the meal, his mouth burned so badly that he demanded water. The children, however, explained that the water in the pot was in three layers, the top for their father, the middle for his second wife and the bottom for his first.

"You lie!" Can't-bear-to-be-contradicted cried, desperate for a drink, and he demanded that Anansi beat his children in punishment. Instead, Anansi ordered the children to beat Can't-bear-to-be-contradicted, and this they did, savagely.

"What right do they have to do this?" Can't-bear-to-be-contradicted screeched as the blows fell.

"Since you hate to be contradicted, you cannot contradict others, yet you have, and that is why I have ordered them to beat you."

Anansi, his wives and children beat Can't-bear-to-be-contradicted so severely that he shattered into tiny pieces, scattering widely across the land, and it is for this reason, the Ashanti say, that so many people simply cannot bear to be contradicted.

Online Resources

Other books about African history by Charles River Editors

Further Reading

Abimbola, Wade (ed. and trans., 1977). Ifa Divination Poetry NOK, New York).

Baldick, Julian (1997). Black God: the Afroasiatic roots of the Jewish, Christian, and Muslim religions. Syracuse University Press:ISBN 0-8156-0522-6

Barnes, Sandra. Africa's Ogun: Old World and New (Bloomington: Indiana University Press, 1989).

Beier, Ulli, ed. The Origins of Life and Death: African Creation Myths (London: Heinemann, 1966).

Bowen, P.G. (1970). Sayings of the Ancient One - Wisdom from Ancient Africa. Theosophical Publishing House, U.S.

Chidester, David. "Religions of South Africa" pp. 17–19

Cole, Herbert Mbari. Art and Life among the Owerri Igbo (Bloomington: Indiana University press, 1982).

Danquah, J. B., The Akan Doctrine of God: A Fragment of Gold Coast Ethics and Religion, second edition (London: Cass, 1968).

Gbadagesin, Segun. African Philosophy: Traditional Yoruba Philosophy and Contemporary African Realities

(New York: Peter Lang, 1999).

Gleason, Judith. Oya, in Praise of an African Goddess (Harper Collins, 1992).

Griaule, Marcel; Dietterlen, Germaine. Le Mythe Cosmogonique (Paris: Institut d'Ethnologie, 1965).

Idowu, Bolaji, God in Yoruba Belief (Plainview: Original Publications, rev. and enlarged ed., 1995)

LaGamma, Alisa (2000). Art and oracle: African art and rituals of divination. New York: The Metropolitan Museum of Art. ISBN 978-0-87099-933-8. Archived from the original on 2013-05-10.

Lugira, Aloysius Muzzanganda. African traditional religion. Infobase Publishing, 2009.

Mbiti, John African Religions and Philosophy (1969) African Writers Series, Heinemann ISBN 0-435-89591-5

Opoku, Kofi Asare (1978). West African Traditional Religion Kofi Asare Opoku | Publisher: FEP International Private Limited. ASIN: B0000EE0IT

Parrinder, Geoffrey. African Traditional Religion, Third ed. (London: Sheldon Press, 1974). ISBN 0-85969-014-8 pbk.

Parrinder, Geoffrey. "Traditional Religion", in his

Africa's Three Religions, Second ed. (London: Sheldon Press, 1976, ISBN 0-85969-096-2), p. [15-96].

Peavy, D., (2009)."Kings, Magic & Medicine". Raleigh, NC: SI.

Peavy, D., (2016). The Benin Monarchy, Olokun & Iha Ominigbon. Umewaen: Journal of Benin & Edoid Studies: Osweego, NY.

Popoola, S. Solagbade. Ikunle Abiyamo: It is on Bent Knees that I gave Birth (2007 Asefin Media Publication)

Soyinka, Wole, Myth, Literature and the African World (Cambridge University Press, 1976).

Alice Werner, Myths and Legends of the Bantu (1933). Available online at sacred-texts.com

Umeasigbu, Rems Nna. The Way We Lived: Ibo Customs and Stories (London: Heinemann, 1969).

Free Books by Charles River Editors

We have brand new titles available for free most days of the week. To see which of our titles are currently free, click on this link.

Discounted Books by Charles River Editors

We have titles at a discount price of just 99 cents everyday. To see which of our titles are currently 99 cents, click on this link.